Role of Constitution in Socio- Economic and Political Justice

Historical Perspective of Constitution:-

People write and adopt constitution because they want to make a fresh start in their system of governance. The constitution represents a break from the past in what it accepts and what it rejects. This is specially so about the constitutions of former colonised countries.

1600 to 1772

The East India Company :-

The British authority in India was established through the agency of a trding corporation- The East India Company- formed in England in 1600 under a charter of Queen Elizabeth I . The company established its trading centres at chiefly Bombay, Calcutta & Madras.

The crown had given to the company certain legislative and judicial powers to be exercised by it over the english servants of the company andsuch indian settlors who placed themselves under its protection. But the laws made by the company were not to be contrary to the laws , stautes of England.

Similar powers were affirmed by the charters granted by James I and Charles II in 1609 and 1661 respectively.

The Company gained a lot of powers in this time by winning the battles of Buxar and plassey.

1773 to 1832

Regulating Act 1773:-

The Act set up a government in Bengal consisting of a governor general and 4 councillors, in whom military and civil government of empire was vested. The Supreme Court in Bengal was established.

The Act of 1781

By this act the Governor General and council were empowered to frame regulations for the provincial courts and coucils. Copies of these regulations were required to be sent to the Court of Directors and the Secretary of State, who might disallow them within two years.

The Charter Act of 1831

By this Act the powers of all three councils were enlarged and simultaneously subjected to greater control by Parliament.

1833 to 1856

Constitutional Changes:-

The Charter act of 1833 introduced important changes in Indian legislation. It vested legislative powers in the Governor General in Council, which consisted of Governor general and four ordinary members. Three members were from within the East India company and one was from outside the Company.

The existing powers of councils of Madras and Bombay were superseded . The executive authority of Governor General in coucil extended to superintendence, direction and control of the whole civil , military government of the company's possession in India.

The Act of 1853:-

The act of 1853 differentiated the legislative machinery from the executive. Under this Act the Governor General in council was enlarged by six new members called legislative members. These were :- The Chief Justice of Bengal, a puisne judge of the supreme Court and four officials appointed by provincial governments. The Governor General was given the veto right in legislative matters.

1857 to 1918

The first war of Indian Independence in 1857 brought the career of East India Company to an end. In 1858 the governement of India was placed directly under the crown through the Secretary of state for India. In 1861 by Councils Act the Governor General Council was reinforced by additional members, between six to twelve, nominated for two years, of whom half were to be non officials. The assent of Governor General was necessary in all legislation.

By the Minto-morley reforms of

1909 the membreships of councils was increased. The number of additional members was fixed at 60 of whom 24 were to be non-officials.

1919 to 1949

The Government of India Act 1919:-

The main features of the Act are :-

(1) It introduced the system of dyarchy in the provinces. In this system the provision was made in the Act for classifying the subjects as Central and Provincial matters.

(2) No principle of responsible government was introduced in the centre. The Government in India remained with the Governor General in Counil, responsible only to united kingdom's Parliament through Secretary of state for India. The powers of both chambers of the Indian

legislature were identical except that the power to vote supply of money was granted only to the legislative assembly. In respect of financial bills the chambers had equal powers.

(3) The structure of government was to remain unitary. The governor General was final authority to decide whether a particular topic was central or provincial matter and not courts.

The Government of India Act 1935:-

The main features of the Act are as follows:-

(1) Statutory Division of Powers-

The act made a division of powers between the centre and the provinces. Certain subjects were assigned exclusively to central or federal legislature, others to the provincial legislatures.

(2) The proposed All India Federation

The Act proposed to substitute a federal system for what was in substance a unitary system of government. The consituent units of the fedration were to be the Governor provinces and Indian states. The accessionof the states to the federation was optional.

Governor's provinces

The executive government of the provinces vested in the governor. The act provided for the responsible government in the provinces subject to following limitations:

(1) Special responsiblities were given to the governor on lines similar to the governor general save as regards finance.

(2) Certain matters were placed outside the ministerial control and relegated to the Governor.

Federal Court

The Act set up a federal Court. It consisted of a Chief Justice and six other judges. an increase over six needed the approval of federal legislature. The judges were appointed by warrant under Royal sign Mannual.

The Cripps Mission 1942:-

The proposals of the cripps mission were as follows:-

(1) Immediately after cessation of hostilities, steps shall be taken to form a indian consititution making body to frame a new constitution for India.

(2) the indian states should participate in the Constitution making body.

(3) Her Majesty's Government would accept and implement the constitution so framed subject only to

(i) the right of any province to refuse to accept

the new constitution and to retain its existing constitutional position

(ii) the signing of a treaty between Her Majesty's government and the constitution making body.

(4) Until the new constitution could be framed, the British governrment would retain the control and direction of defence of india as part of world war effort..

(5) The leaders of the parties were invited to join the viceroy governemnt.

        The negotiations broke down because of the differences of congress and muslim league.

The Wavell plan 1945:-

This plan introduced by viceroy Viscount Wavell failed because no agreement could be arrived at regarding the composition of the proposed executive council.

Indian Independence Act:-

The main provisions of this Act introduced by Viceroy Lord Mountbatten are as follows:-

(1) It set up two independent dominions in India known as India and Pakistan respectively.

(2) In each dominion there was to be a Governor General who was to be appointed by the King.

(3) The legislatures of the new dominions were to have full legislative sovereignity, and no act of the british parliament passed after August 15,1947, was to extend to either of the new dominions as a part of the law of that dominion unless it was extended thereto by a law of the legislature of that dominion.

(4) After August 15,1947, the british government were to have no responsiblity, respecting the government of India or Pakistan.

(5) The paramountcy of the British Crown over the Indian states was to lapse.

(6) The powers of the legislatures of the dominion were exercisable by the constituent Assembly. The Consatituent Assembly was not to be subject to any limitation whatsoever in exercising its constituent powers.

(7) Until a new constitution was framed the government of India Act 1935, subject to certain adaptations and modifications was to remain constitutional law of India

Form of Constitution:-

A constitution which embodies a federal system has normally the following five characterstics:-

(1) Distribution of Powers:-

An essential feature of every

federal constitution is the distribution of powers between the Central Government and the Governments of the several units forming the federation. Federation means the distribution of powers of state among a number of coordinate bodies, each originating in and controlled by the Constitution.

(2) Supremacy of the Constitution:-

This means that the constitution should be binding on the federal and state governments.

(3) Written Constitution:-

The Constitution must almost necessarily be written CConstitution.

(4) Rigidity:-

It means that powers of amending the Constitution, regarding those provisions which regulate the status and powers of the federal and state governments should not be confided exclusively either to the federal or state governments.

(5) Authority of Courts:-

    This involves two connected matters. Firstly there must be some authority, normally the courts of law, which can prevent the federal and state governments from encroaching upon each others powers and declare laws made by them as ultra vires on the ground of excess of powers. The Supreme Court should have the authority to have last words in matters involving constitutional interpretation.

Introduction:-

    The role of Executive Legislature and Judiciary in Socio- Economic and political Justice in India is of utmost significance. Prior to the enactment of constitution, during British rule, the whole country was governed by British Parliament with little autonomy to some indian politicians and parties. The Britishers needed Indians only for clerical jobs and all the big posts were reserved for native britishers.

When the Britishers went back to uk after their stay in India, they were known as nabobs because of the huge wealth that they had amassed during their stay in India. After independence constitution was enacted. It was based on many constitutions with most of the features of unwritten constitution of the uk. Our parliamentary system resembles closely to British parliament with crown replaced by President.

(I) Role of Executive in Socio- Economic and Political Justice in INDIA

The executive branch is one of the three branches of government which are central to the institutional design of Constitution. The allocation of powers and interrelation between the three branches of government :- The executive, legislature and judiciaryare key elements of such a structure. According to Aristotle there are three types of functions of government:-

(1) Deliberative   (2) Magesterial
    (3) Judicial.

According to Wade and Phillips the doctrine of Seperation of power implies:-

(1) The same person should not form more than one organ of government.

(2) One organ of government should not exercise the functions of other organs of the government

(3) One organ of the government should not encroach with the function of other two organs of government.

        Beyond the broad and general distinction that that the legislature makes the laws and approves the budget the executive implements the laws and the judiciary adjudicates upon the law , many questions need to be addressed and answered in order to design the appropriate balance between the three. There are three types systems of government as follows:-

(1) Presidential System

(2) Parliamentary System

(3) Mixed System

(1) Presidential System:-

    (a) In this system the executive and legislature are seperate agents of electorate and their origin and survival are thus seperated.

    (b) The President is both the head of the state and head of the government.

    (c) The President is elected by popular vote(or by an intermediate institution that carries out the popular preferences)

(d) The President office of term is fixed. He/she is neither politically accountable to the legislature nor dependent on his/her party's support to stay in office.

(e) Generally the cabinet derives its authority exclusively from the president

(f) Often the President has some political impact in the process of law making

(II) Parlimentary System:-

(a) The key criterion is the fusion of powers; the executive is hierarchically subordinated to the legislature.

(b) The head of the government is elected by the legislature.

(c) The head of the government is accountable to parliament(through a vote of no confidence) and dependent on his/her party's support.

(d) Generally the head of state is not the same person as the head of government.

(III) Mixed System:-

(a) the key characterstic of a mixed system is a dual executive . It combines a transactional relationship between the executiveand the legislature with a hierarchical one.

(b) the President who serves as the head of the state is elected by the popular vote.

(c) Neither the President nor the legislature is in full control of selecting/appointing and removing the prime minister.

(d) Generally , the president possesses quite considerale executive powers.

The Form of government :-

The constitution sets up parliamentary governments both in the centre and the states. Parliamentary government embodies the following essentials:-

(1) The presence of nominal executive head of the state who acts exclusively on the advice of Council of Ministers or Cabinet. The nominal executive may be hereditary asthe King in England, elected as President in Federal Republic of Germany, or appointed as the Governor General in a Dominion.

(2) The Cabinet which is the real executive consists of leaders of a party, or a coalition of parties, who have the support of majority in the legislature. This group of men agrees to pursue a common policy under a common leader, namelt the Prime Minister.

(3) The Prime Minister occupies a dominant position in the Cabinet. He appoints Ministers and assigns them to their Offices. He can

dismiss anyone of them. "The Cabinet is the steering of the ship of state but the steersman is prime minister.

(4) The tenure of the office of the Cabinet is dependent on the will of the legislature, but if the legislature consists of two houses , on support of the lower house.This means that ministry which has lost the confidence of legislature must retire from the office. A government remains in office so long as its policy has the approval of the legislature.

(5) THe responsiblity of the Cabinet is collective. The Cabinet acts as body.Ministers stand and fall togather.From this it follows that that the cabinet must in all circumstances, agree,. If there is disagreement among the ministers, either the Cabinet as a whole or the dissenting minister must resign.

(6) The parliamentary government works by interaction of four essential factors:

(i) the principle of majority rule.

(ii) The willingness of minority for the time being to accept the decision of the majority.

(iii) The existence of great political parties divided by broad issues of policy, rather than by sectional interest.

(iv) The existence of mobile body of political opinion, owing no permanent allegiance to any party.

I.—THE EXECUTIVE

The President and Vice-President

52. The President of India.—There shall be a President of India.

53. Executive power of the Union.—(1) The executive power of the Union shall be vested in the President and shall be exercised by him either directly or through officers subordinate to him in accordance with this Constitution.

(2) Without prejudice to the generality of the

foregoing provision, the supreme command of the Defence Forces of the Union shall be vested in the President and the exercise thereof shall be regulated by law.

(3) Nothing in this article shall—

(a) be deemed to transfer to the President any functions conferred by any existing law on the Government of any State or other authority; or

(b) prevent Parliament from conferring by law functions on authorities other than the President.

54. Election of President.—The President shall be elected by the members of an electoral college consisting of—

(a) the elected members of both Houses of Parliament; and

(b) the elected members of the Legislative Assemblies of the States.

Explanation.—In this article and in article 55, "State" includes the National Capital Territory of Delhi and the Union territory of Pondicherry.

55. Manner of election of President. —(1) As

far as practicable, there shall be uniformity in the scale of representation of the different States at the election of the President.

(2) For the purpose of securing such uniformity among the States inter se as well as parity between the States as a whole and the Union, the number of votes which each elected member of Parliament and of the Legislative Assembly of each State is entitled to cast at such election shall be determined in the following manner:—

(a) every elected member of the Legislative Assembly of a State shall have as many votes as there are multiples of one thousand in the quotient obtained by dividing the population of the State by the total number of the elected members of the Assembly;

(b) if, after taking the said multiples of one thousand, the remainder is not less than five hundred, then the vote of each member referred to in sub-clause (a) shall be further increased by one;

(c) each elected member of either House of Parliament shall have such number of votes as may be obtained by dividing the total number of votes assigned to the members of the Legislative Assemblies of the States under sub-clauses (a) and (b) by the total number of the elected members of both Houses of Parliament, fractions exceeding one-half being counted as one and other fractions being disregarded.

(3) The election of the President shall be held in accordance with the system of proportional representation by means of the single transferable vote and the voting at such election shall be by secret ballot.

Explanation.— In this article, the expression "population" means the population as ascertained at the last preceding census of which the relevant figures have been published:

Provided that the reference in this Explanation to the last preceding census of which the relevant figures have been published shall, until the relevant figures for the first census taken after the year 2026 have been published, be construed as a reference to the 1971 census.

56. Term of office of President.—(1) The President shall hold office for a term of five years from the date on which he enters upon his office:

Provided that—

(a) the President may, by writing under his hand addressed to the Vice-President, resign his office;

(b) the President may, for violation of the Constitution, be removed from office by impeachment in the manner provided in article 61;

(c) the President shall, notwithstanding the

expiration of his term, continue to hold office until his successor enters upon his office.

(2) Any resignation addressed to the Vice-President under clause (a) of the proviso to clause (1) shall forthwith be communicated by him to the Speaker of the House of the People.

57. Eligibility for re-election.—A person who holds, or who has held, office as President shall, subject to the other provisions of this Constitution, be eligible for re-election to that office.

58. Qualifications for election as President.—(1) No person shall be eligible for election as President unless he—

    (a) is a citizen of India,

    (b) has completed the age of thirty-five years, and

    (c) is qualified for election as a member of the House of the People.

(2) A person shall not be eligible for election as President if he holds any office of profit under the Government of India or the Government of any State or under any local or other authority

subject to the control of any of the said Governments.

Explanation.—For the purposes of this article, a person shall not be

74. Council of Ministers to aid and advise President.—(1) There shall be a Council of Ministers with the Prime Minister at the head to aid and advise the President who shall, in the exercise of his functions, act in accordance with such advice:

Provided that the President may require the Council of Ministers to reconsider such advice, either generally or otherwise, and the President shall act in accordance with the advice tendered after such reconsideration.

(2) The question whether any, and if so what, advice was tendered by Ministers to the President shall not be inquired into in any court.

75. Other provisions as to Ministers.—(1) The Prime Minister shall be appointed by the President and the other Ministers shall be appointed by the President on the advice of the

Prime Minister.

(1A) The total number of Ministers, including the Prime Minister, in the Council of Ministers shall not exceed fifteen per cent. of the total number of members of the House of the People.

(1B) A member of either House of Parliament belonging to any political party who is disqualified for being a member of that House under paragraph 2 of the Tenth Schedule shall also be disqualified to be appointed as a Minister under clause (1) for duration of the period commencing from the date of his disqualification till the date on which the term of his office as such member would expire or where he contests any election to either House of Parliament before the expiry of such period, till the date on which he is declared elected, whichever is earlier.

(2) The Ministers shall hold office during the pleasure of the President.

(3) The Council of Ministers shall be collectively responsible to the House of the

People.

(4) Before a Minister enters upon his office, the President shall administer to him the oaths of office and of secrecy according to the forms set out for the purpose in the Third Schedule.

(5) A Minister who for any period of six consecutive months is not a member of either House of Parliament shall at the expiration of that period cease to be a Minister.

(6) The salaries and allowances of Ministers shall be such as Parliament may from time to time by law determine and, until Parliament so determines, shall be as specified in the Second Schedule.

79. Constitution of Parliament.—There shall be a Parliament for the Union which shall consist of the President and two Houses to be known respectively as the Council of States and the House of the People.

80. Composition of the Council of States.—(1)

The Council of States shall consist of—

(a) twelve members to be nominated by the President in accordance with the provisions of clause (3); and

(b) not more than two hundred and thirty-eight representatives of the States and of the Union territories.

(2) The allocation of seats in the Council of States to be filled by representatives of the States and of the Union territories shall be in accordance with the provisions in that behalf contained in the Fourth Schedule.

(3) The members to be nominated by the President under sub-clause (a) of clause (1) shall consist of persons having special knowledge or practical experience in respect of such matters as the following, namely:—

Literature, science, art and social service.

(4) The representatives of each State in the Council of States shall be elected by the elected members of the Legislative Assembly of the State in accordance with the system of proportional representation by means of the single transferable vote.

(5) The representatives of the Union territories in the Council of States shall be chosen in such manner as Parliament may by law prescribe.

81. Composition of the House of the People.—(1) Subject to the provisions of article 331, the House of the People shall consist of—

(a) not more than five hundred and thirty members chosen by direct election from territorial constituencies in the States, and

(b) not more than twenty members to represent the Union territories, chosen in such manner as Parliament may by law provide.

(2) For the purposes of sub-clause (a) of clause (1),—

(a) there shall be allotted to each State a number of seats in the House of the People in such manner that the ratio between that number and the population of the State is, so far as practicable, the same for all States; and

(b) each State shall be divided into territorial constituencies in such manner that the ratio between the population of each constituency and the number of seats allotted to it is, so far as practicable, the same throughout the State:

Provided that the provisions of sub-clause (a) of this clause shall not be applicable for the purpose of allotment of seats in the House of the People to any State so long as the population of that State does not exceed six millions.

(3) In this article, the expression "population" means the population as ascertained at the last preceding census of which the relevant figures have been published:

Provided that the reference in this clause to the last preceding census of which the relevant figures have been published shall, until the relevant figures for the first census taken after the year 2026 have been published, be construed, —

(i) for the purposes of sub-clause (a) of clause (2) and the proviso to that clause, as a reference to the 1971 census; and

(ii) for the purposes of sub-clause (b) of clause (2) as a reference to the 2001 census.

82. Readjustment after each census.—Upon the completion of each census, the allocation of seats in the House of the People to the States and the division of each State into territorial constituencies shall be readjusted by such authority and in such manner as Parliament may by law determine:

Provided that such readjustment shall not affect representation in the House of the People until the dissolution of the then existing House:

Provided further that such readjustment shall take effect from such date as the President may, by order, specify and until such readjustment takes effect, any election to the House may be held on the basis of the territorial constituencies existing before such readjustment:

Provided also that until the relevant figures for the first census taken after the year 2026 have been published, it shall not be necessary to readjust—

(i) the allocation of seats in the House of

People to the States as readjusted on the basis of the 1971 census; and

(ii) the division of each State into territorial constituencies as may be readjusted on the basis of the 2001 census,

under this article.

83. Duration of Houses of Parliament.—(1) The Council of States shall not be subject to dissolution, but as nearly as possible one-third of the members thereof shall retire as soon as may be on the expiration of every second year in accordance with the provisions made in that behalf by Parliament by law.

(2) The House of the People, unless sooner dissolved, shall continue for five years from the date appointed for its first meeting and no longer and the expiration of the said period of five years shall operate as a dissolution of the House:

Provided that the said period may, while a Proclamation of Emergency is in operation, be extended by Parliament by law for a period not exceeding one year at a time and not extending in any case beyond a period of six months after the Proclamation has ceased to operate.

84. Qualification for membership of Parliament.—A person shall not be qualified to be chosen to fill a seat in Parliament unless he—

(a) is a citizen of India, and makes and subscribes before some person authorised in that behalf by the Election Commission an oath or affirmation according to the form set out for the purpose in the Third Schedule;

(b) is, in the case of a seat in the Council of States, not less than thirty years of age and, in the case of a seat in the House of the People, not less than twenty- five years of age; and

(c) possesses such other qualifications as may be prescribed in that behalf by or under any law made by Parliament.

85. Sessions of Parliament, prorogation and dissolution.—(1) The President shall from time to time summon each House of Parliament to meet at such time and place as he thinks fit, but six months shall not intervene between its last sitting in one session and the date appointed for its first sitting in the next session.

(2) The President may from time to time—

(a) prorogue the Houses or either House;

(b) dissolve the House of the People.

86. Right of President to address and send messages to Houses.—(1) The President may address either House of Parliament or both Houses

Establishment and constitution of Supreme Court.—(1) There shall be a Supreme Court of India consisting of a Chief Justice of India and, until Parliament by law prescribes a larger number, of not more than seven1 other Judges.

(2) Every Judge of the Supreme Court shall be appointed by the President by warrant under his hand and seal after consultation with such of the Judges of the Supreme Court and of the High Courts in the States as the President may

deem necessary for the purpose and shall hold office until he attains the age of sixty-five years:

Provided that in the case of appointment of a Judge other than the Chief Justice, the Chief Justice of India shall always be consulted:

Provided further that—

(a) a Judge may, by writing under his hand addressed to the President, resign his office;

(b) a Judge may be removed from his office in the manner provided in clause (4).

(2A) The age of a Judge of the Supreme Court shall be determined by such authority and in such manner as Parliament may by law provide.

(3) A person shall not be qualified for appointment as a Judge of the Supreme Court unless he is a citizen of India and—

(a) has been for at least five years a Judge of a High Court or of two or more such Courts in succession; or

(b) has been for at least ten years an advocate of a High Court or of two or more such Courts in succession; or

(c) is, in the opinion of the President, a distinguished jurist.

Explanation I.—In this clause "High Court" means a High Court which exercises, or which at any time before the commencement of this Constitution exercised, jurisdiction in any part of the territory of India.

Explanation II.—In computing for the purpose of this clause the period during which a person has been an advocate, any period during which a person has held judicial office not inferior to that of a district judge after he became an advocate shall be included.

(4) A Judge of the Supreme Court shall not be removed from his office except by an order of

the President passed after an address by each House of Parliament supported by a majority of the total membership of that House and by a majority of not less than two-thirds of the members of that House present and voting has been presented to the President in the same session for such removal on the ground of proved misbehaviour or incapacity.

(5) Parliament may by law regulate the procedure for the presentation of an address and for the investigation and proof of the misbehaviour or incapacity of a Judge under clause (4).

(6) Every person appointed to be a Judge of the Supreme Court shall, before he enters upon his office, make and subscribe before the President, or some person appointed in that behalf by him, an oath or affirmation according to the form set out for the purpose in the Third Schedule.

(7) No person who has held office as a Judge of the Supreme Court shall plead or act in any court or before any authority within the territory of India.

125. Salaries, etc., of Judges.—(1) There shall be paid to the Judges of the Supreme Court such salaries as may be determined by Parliament by law and, until provision in that behalf is so made, such salaries as are specified in the Second Schedule.

(2) Every Judge shall be entitled to such privileges and allowances and to such rights in respect of leave of absence and pension as may from time to time be determined by or under law made by Parliament and, until so determined, to such privileges, allowances and rights as are specified in the Second Schedule:

Provided that neither the privileges nor the allowances of a Judge nor his rights in respect of leave of absence or pension shall be varied to his disadvantage after his appointment.

126. Appointment of acting Chief Justice.—When the office of Chief Justice of India is vacant or when the Chief Justice is, by reason of absence or otherwise, unable to perform the duties of his office, the duties of the office shall be performed by such one of the other Judges of the Court as the President may appoint for the purpose.

127. Appointment of ad hoc Judges.—(1) If at any time there should not be a quorum of the Judges of the Supreme Court available to hold or continue any session of the Court, the Chief Justice of India may, with the previous consent of the President and after consultation with the Chief Justice of the High Court concerned, request in writing the attendance at the sittings of the Court, as an ad hoc Judge, for such period as may be necessary, of a Judge of a High Court duly qualified for appointment as a Judge of the

Supreme Court to be designated by the Chief Justice of India.

(2) It shall be the duty of the Judge who has been so designated, in priority to other duties of his office, to attend the sittings of the Supreme Court at the time and for the period for which his attendance is required, and while so attending he shall have all the jurisdiction, powers and privileges, and shall discharge the duties, of a Judge of the Supreme Court.

128. Attendance of retired Judges at sittings of the Supreme Court.—Notwithstanding anything in this Chapter, the Chief Justice of India may at any time, with the previous consent of the President, request any person who has held the office of a Judge of the Supreme Court or of the Federal Court or who has held the office of a Judge of a High Court and is duly qualified for appointment as a Judge of the Supreme Court to sit and act as a Judge of the Supreme Court,

and every such person so requested shall, while so sitting and acting, be entitled to such allowances as the President may by order determine and have all the jurisdiction, powers and privileges of, but shall not otherwise be deemed to be, a Judge of that Court:

Provided that nothing in this article shall be deemed to require any such person as aforesaid to sit and act as a Judge of that Court unless he consents so to do.

129. Supreme Court to be a court of record.—The Supreme Court shall be a court of record and shall have all the powers of such a court including the power to punish for contempt of itself.

130. Seat of Supreme Court.—The Supreme Court shall sit in Delhi or in such other place or places, as the Chief Justice of India may, with the approval of the President, from time to time, appoint.

131. Original jurisdiction of the Supreme Court.—Subject to the provisions of this Constitution, the Supreme Court shall, to the exclusion of any other court, have original jurisdiction in any dispute—

(a) between the Government of India and one or more States; or

(b) between the Government of India and any State or States on one side and one or more other States on the other; or

(c) between two or more States,

if and in so far as the dispute involves any question (whether of law or fact) on which the existence or extent of a legal right depends:

Provided that the said jurisdiction shall not extend to a dispute arising out of any treaty, agreement, covenant, engagement, sanad or other similar instrument which, having been entered into or executed before the commencement of this Constitution, continues in operation after such commencement, or which provides that the said jurisdiction shall not extend to such a dispute.

131A. [Exclusive jurisdiction of the Supreme Court in regard to questions as to constitutional validity of Central laws.] Rep. by the Constitution (Forty-third Amendment) Act, 1977, s. 4 (w.e.f. 13-4-1978).

Seperation of Powers:-

The doctrine of seperation of powers stated in its rigid form means that each of the powers of government namely executive, legislative and judicial should should be confined exclusively to a seperate department or organs of government. There should be no overlapping either of functions or of individual. The US constitution is the best example of seperation of powers. While the US constitution does not expressly provide for seperation of powers, the doctrine has been incorporated in the constitution by the provision that " all legislative powers shall be vested in the Congress". Article 1 Section 1 ;"The executive power shall be vested in the President", Article 2 Section 1 ;"THe judicial powers shall be vested in one Supreme Court and in such inferior courts as congress may from time to time ordain and establish".

Under Indian constitution only executive power is "vested" in the president while provisions are made for a parliament and judiciary without expressly vesting the legislative and judicial powers in any person or body. Moreover we have the same system of Parliamentary executive as in England and the Council of Minsters consisting as it does of the members of legislaturesis , like the British cabinet, "a hyphen which joins the buckle which fastens the legislative part of the state to the executive part."

Indian constitution provides for independent judiciary with extensive jurisdiction over acts of legislature and the executive

A history of the doctrine of judicial independence

The genesis of the doctrine of judicial independence is to be found in the evolution of a constitutional democratic state in Europe. It is accompanied by the development of the rule of law, with the attendant prerequisites of the separation of powers and the existence of checks and balances. The debate about the role of the courts in general and the judges in particular evolved in the context of the history of the exercise of unfettered power by political rulerships, mainly in Great Britain, but also later in the United States and Europe.

Historically, the institutional and normative conditions that precipitated the evolution of a constitutional or democratic system operated in Europe in two distinct ways: as a product of the yoke of absolutism, and as the antithesis of unfettered power. The collapse of the feudal system and the unification of nation states based on large political territories under absolutist monarchs generated national economies and political systems that needed a different type of law and order. Conditions arose that led to the emergence of a new mercantile bourgeoisie. At the same time, the interference of absolute monarchs in trade created conflict with this emerging bourgeois society which nurtured new expectations of its own. Importantly, this context of struggle by the bourgeoisie against the old doctrines, such as that of divine rights which justified absolutist rule and unlimited powers, generated a slew of political and constitutional debates that in turn set the pace for constitutional systems.

The rule of law emerged to limit the whims of rulers by subordinating their acts to the law. In its general application, it ensured that citizens, the state and its institutions – including, of course, the monarch – were all subjected to the supremacy of the law. The rule of law formed the basis of a state strong enough to secure order and free commercial activity, but one limited in its competence by the restrictions of the law.

In its political sense, the rule of law signified a landmark transformation of the absolutist state to a liberal constitutional state. This was a state born of the political victory of the bourgeoisie against the exclusive political power of the monarchs. Economically, the laissez-faire spirit was replaced by a new state of affairs wherein a power derived from a contract, and power was to be shared between the upper and middle ranks of society together with the ruler. This was to become the constitutional system in a democratic system of governance.

It is against this background, therefore, that traditional scholars of constitutional theory regard the original edifi ce of constitutionalism as the subordination of the exercise of governmental power to legal rules.

Most constitutional law experts would concur that the independence of the judiciary is only possible in a constitutional democracy that involves the proposition and appreciation that the exercise of governmental power is bounded by rules: rules that prescribe the procedures according to which legislative and executive acts are to be performed, and delimit their permissible content.4

In simple terms, this background was as follows: the King of England did not hear cases himself; therefore, he depended upon certain people to do so on his behalf, and in his name. The King's representatives did not have their own minds, so to speak, but stood in for the King and reported directly to him. The decisions they made were his decisions, which, once he was satisfied with them, could not be questioned. Over a period, the role of the interpretive courts evolved into a separate institution altogether.

The struggle to limit monarchical powers in the history of Great Britain continued for a long period since the issue of separating legislative, executive and judicial powers in England was not an easy one, particularly because the British have never developed a written constitution. It was only with the seizure of power from King William in a coup d'état in 1668, when legislative powers were stripped away from the absolute monarch, that it became possible to wrest power away from the one person who had until then been the maker, interpreter and enforcer of the law. The settlement – which allowed him to return to the throne – was the agreement that Parliament would henceforth make the laws, albeit in the name of the King. From then onwards, the British King became more and more of a figurehead, functionally speaking.

The country whose constitutional history has a more direct bearing on the modern judicial independence debate is the United States of America (USA). The American experience commenced as a rebellion from the established British and other European systems of absolute power in the hands of one person or a system. The USA as we know it was predicated upon the desire to establish and commit itself to creating a constitutional system with clear checks and balances among the three organs of government. Alexander Hamilton, one of the framers of the American Constitution, wrote the following in defence of the independence of the judiciary in the constitutional

... there is no liberty, if the power of judging be not separated from the legislative and executive powers ...

American President Woodrow Wilson (1913–1921) argued that government –6

... keeps its promises, or does not keep them, in its courts ... The struggle for constitutional government is a struggle for good laws, indeed, but also for intelligent, independent and impartial courts ...

Following this, and in subsequent court rulings and political utterances, American opinion-makers have been consistent in their defence of the judiciary. In *Brown versus the Board of Education* (1954), a landmark decision, the United States Supreme Court declared that the existing separation of education facilities for children of different race groups was inherently unequal and unconstitutional.

Some of the cornerstones of judicial independence follow, for consideration:[3]

(1) Judges are free to evaluate, objectively, the facts of the disputes placed before them by applying the constitution, existing laws and ordinances objectively and without duress from other organs of government

(2) The judicial arm of the state operates independently vis-à-vis the legislative and executive spheres of the same socio-political system which created them all

(3) Officers of the courts are independent from one another, and seniority in terms of the judicial hierarchy does not affect their judgement in relation to one another

(4) All matters of a judicial nature are attended to by competent members of the legal fraternity

(5) Assignment of judges to handle cases is undertaken by senior officials of the court solely on clear and convincing

evidence of their ability to perform the required tasks
(6) Tenure of judges lasts until retirement in terms of conditions established by appointed members of the legal enterprise
(7) The state allocates sufficient financial and other resources to the judiciary to obviate temptations that arise as a result of financial insecurity
(8) Disciplinary action against judges is taken solely on convincing grounds of inability to perform, and
(9) The selection and appointment of judges is purely on selective criteria in accordance with the merit system.

Indian Judiciary, Judicial review and activism

An independent and impartial judiciary is said to be first condition of liberty. It is custodian of the rights of the citizens. In a fedral constitution, it plays another important role ; it dtermines the limit of powers of the Centre and the state.

The following provisions of the constitution are intended to secure independence and impartiality of the supreme court and High Courts.

(1) The President appoints the judges after consultation with judicial authorities. In case of appointment of Chief Justice of India, the President must consult such judges of the supreme court as he may deem necessary. For the selection of other judges of the Supreme Court he muist consult the Chief Justice of India(CJI). The appoinement of the High Court judges will be made by president after consultation with the CJI and Governor of the state. In the case of appointment of other judges of any High Court the President must consult the CJ of concerned High Court. Thus in appoinment of judges the , the constitution does not give absolute discretion to the executive.

(2) Security of tenure is guaranteed to every judge. A judge of the High Court or Supreme Court can be removed on the ground of proved misbehavior or incapacity. The President can only remove a judge only when an address has been presented to him against that judge by each house of Parliament.

(3) Salaries of judges have been fixed by the constitution and cannot be varied by legislature except during the financial emergency. Once appointed, their privileges, rights and allowances cannot be altered to their disadvantage.

(4) The Supreme Court and high Courts have been given the authority to recruit their staff and frame rules regarding conditions of service.

(5) Expenditure in respect of the salaries and allowances of the judges is not put to vote of legislatures.

(6) The administrative staff of the supreme court, including salaries, allowances and pensions, payable to its officers are charged on the Consolidated Fund of India. Similarly the administrative expenses of the High Court are charged on the Consolidated fund of the State.

(7) The Constitution debars the Supreme Court judges from pleading or appearing before any court or judicial authority in India even after retirement. Also after retirement a judge of the High Court can practice only in the Supreme Court or in a High Court in which he has not been a judge.

(8) No discusion shall take place in the legislature of a state or Parliament with respect to the conduct of any judge of the Supreme Court or of a High Court in the discharge of their duties

www.ingramcontent.com/pod-product-compliance
Lightning Source LLC
Chambersburg PA
CBHW071814170526
45167CB00003B/1308